Road Rabble

Road Rabble

A Street Memoir of the Seventies

Morgan M. Morgan

With

Eric Leif Davin

DavinBooks
P.O. Box 90087
Pittsburgh, PA 15224

Road Rabble
A Street Memoir of the Seventies

**Cover: Morgan on the Road
Photo by Eric Leif Davin**

Dedication

To my beautiful wife, Abbe, who completes me. To our children, Aric, Ian, Vanessa, Caitlin, Cole, and Cassidy, who fulfill my life. To our grandchildren, Leia, Olivia, Amyia, Dalia, and Lamarie. To our great-grandchildren, Le'Aiylah, Aviannah, Ajalei, and Lillyanna, who bring such joy.

Also, to Lobo, my partner for all those years on the streets, and who traveled all those miles with me.

And to my brothers, especially Eric Leif Davin, who kept pushing me to get my memoirs written before I die. His help with writing, editing, typing, and morale boosting made it all possible.

And, lastly, to my brothers and sisters on the streets, especially the STP Family. Brothers and Sisters to the end.

VENCEREMOS!

Song of the Open Road

We were nearing the end of the road, but we didn't realize it at the time. One seldom does.

The hippie in the old milk truck who picked us all up in Boston dumped us out on the turnpike somewhere down in Connecticut. That was as far as he was going. Fine with us. One place was just as good as someplace else, just so we could hitch a ride.

So, our entire motley tribe of street vagabonds tumbled out of the milk truck onto the side of the road. We watched the milk truck disappear in the distance and then conferred on how best to continue our trek westward. We knew it wasn't likely that another hippie in an old milk truck would drive by and pick us all up. There were over half-a-dozen of us, and we all looked pretty scuzzy. The girls all had big rings in their nostrils at a time when no one wore nose rings. All of us were dressed in rough leather, feathers, pouches, and necklaces of teeth around our necks, whatever. We looked like a band of wandering gypsies; we were road rabble. We decided it'd be best if we split up into smaller groups and rendezvous out West.

So, we split into three groups and let each group get a ride before the next group stepped up to the curb and stuck out their thumbs. That was the last time I saw some of those guys for quite a while. The first group included Juan Valez and Kay, a minister's daughter gone wild. She was originally from Tempe, Arizona, but had hooked up with us up at Earth People's Park. Lobo, a girl named Cocaine, and Black

Barry were in the second group to go. (There were several guys around named "Barry," which led to some confusion when people asked which "Barry" we were talking about. We'd have to say, "You know, the black Barry," so eventually that just became his name.)

I was in the last group, along with Sally and a girl named "Maybe," who'd joined us back in Cambridge. She was a local suburban teen who started hanging with us in Harvard Square. We never knew if she was really street people, or just a townie. Maybe she was, maybe she wasn't, so I nicknamed her "Maybe."

I didn't mind being in the last group, as I figured it'd be easy enough to catch a ride with two girls as my hitching companions. It was November, 1973, and it was cold as a witch's tit as we stood there on the side of the road in the snow. We stuck out our thumbs and hoped a warm ride would come along soon. Sure enough, we soon got a ride that took us all the way to somewhere in Pennsylvania.

We stood by the road for a while, hoping for another quick ride. We got that ride, but it was with a state trooper. The statie pulled over and stopped just beyond us. Then, still sitting inside his nice warm car, he motioned for us to approach. We picked up our packs and trudged up to the passenger side of the statie's car. When we got there he rolled down his window and told us to get in the back. I heard the click as he unlocked the back door and we did as we were told. We tossed in our packs and climbed in next to them. As soon as we were all in, I heard the click of the door locks again, and I knew we were now in the statie's mobile jail cell. I was cold and hungry and in no mood to be hassled by the law, but there wasn't much we could do about the situation.

As it turned out, the statie wasn't going to run us in, after all. Instead, he drove us down the highway to what he said was the end of his patrol area and dropped us off at a small café just off the highway. He gave us each a dollar and told us to go inside, get some coffee, and warm up. He waved to us from inside his car as he made a U-Turn and drove back the way he came. We waved back, then picked up our packs and walked into the café.

We were greeted by hoots and hollers and whistles and shouts of, "Look at the damn hippies!" as soon as we entered. I searched out the directions of the catcalls, ready to fight, and saw they were all coming from a table around which sat Lobo, Black Barry, and Cocaine, all laughing at us and pounding their table. We broke out in smiles, and walked over, damned glad to see them. They kicked out some chairs for us and we joined them at their table.

Usually we enjoyed freaking out the straights by playing up our weirdness and doing deliberately outrageous things, just for the hell of it. Sometimes, sitting in a restaurant like that, I'd stick a cigarette up my nose and smoke it that way. Whatever. Once, back in Cambridge's Riverside neighborhood, Cocaine and I walked up and down River Street dressed as freak-out as we could. I wore a dress and two Pepsi cans strapped around my chest as tits; Cocaine wore a jock strap, a leather vest, a cowboy hat and cowboy boots, and nothing else. The straights stood aside and gawked at us as we sauntered down the street laughing like hyenas. Tonight, though, we were all just pleased to be in a nice warm place on a cold and dark winter night, drinking hot black coffee and eating slices of pie, so we behaved ourselves.

After catching up each other on our rides, I pulled my guitar out of my case and tuned up for some tunes. Somewhere along the way Lobo had obtained a mouth harp, so he joined along with me and we sang some Dylan songs. The other people in the café, mostly truckers, didn't seem to mind, and neither did the waitress. She brought us all free coffee refills and we sat there singing and drinking and staying warm for a long time.

As the sun began to come up we figured we'd best head out on the road, so we gathered up our gear, thanked the waitress for the free coffee, and trekked back out to the highway. Since Lobo, Black Barry, and Cocaine had reached our little oasis first, they stuck out their thumbs first. They soon got a ride, and then we took their spot and stuck out our thumbs. After about an hour of cars and trucks whizzing past, a guy stopped for us and we all piled in.

After about a hundred miles down the road, deeper into the heart of Pennsylvania, our ride let us out at a big truck stop. We decided to go inside and grab some coffee and warm up for a bit. As we walked inside, we were greeted by familiar jeers and catcalls. We looked around and, sonuvabitch, if it wasn't Lobo and Black Barry and Cocaine sitting at a table and laughing at us! The odds of getting two different rides to the very same truck stop two different times must have been overwhelming. We wondered if this was going to happen all across the country.

We sat there for a while, drinking coffee and getting warm and then headed out to the highway again. Since Lobo and the others had gotten to the truck stop first, we let them catch the first ride out of there. It took a long time for us to catch a ride, but when we did, it took us down the road to the western border of Pennsylvania. Our ride dropped us off around three in the morning at another anonymous truck stop. It was cold as hell, and we decided not to try catching another ride right away. We'd have better luck once morning came.

We trudged into the truck stop café, and were immediately greeted with raucous laughter. There sat Lobo, Black Barry, and Cocaine again, slapping their table and pointing at us! This seemed like more than mere coincidence, and we were beginning to freak. What was going on here? What was the cosmic significance of this?

Lobo & Co. had already established friendly relations with the waitresses, so they let us all retreat to the back room where only truckers were allowed. Perhaps they were glad to do this, as it moved our tribe of ruffians from the main dining room to a less visible locale. No one was in the back room, so we just took over the place, plopping down our packs and sprawling all over the floor. Cocaine claimed the pool table as her bed and was soon totally zonked out on it.

We were camped out in the back room for about an hour when the owner walked in and began freaking out to find some barbarian tribe camped out on his floor. He told us to get the hell out, so we gathered up our gear and headed back out into the cold and dark. Just across from the truck stop was a Holiday Inn with a fleet of yellow school busses parked in the lot. We ambled over, pushed open the door to one of the busses, and climbed in. We each claimed a double pair of seats and, despite the bone-chillingly cold night, we were all soon snoring away.

We rousted ourselves in the frosty light of dawn and tumbled out of the school bus before anyone came to kick us out. We let Lobo and his companions take the first ride, then we stuck out our own thumbs. We got a ride all the way to Kansas City and didn't run into Lobo and his ilk anymore. Perhaps the cosmos had finished playing with us.

After that we got a ride that dumped us outside a small farm town just before Wichita. We were having no luck at all until an old farmer who looked like Elmer Fudd in a beat up farm pickup truck stopped and told us to get in. He said he could take us a mite down the road to a better place to catch a ride.

So, we piled into his cab and, as he drove, Elmer Fudd began to ask the usual questions we always got: Where were we coming from, where were we going, why were we on the road, what was it like being on the road? I did most of the talking, trying to answer the farmer's questions as best I could. After about a 45-minute drive, he pulled over and said, "Well, this is a better place for you to catch a ride than the other place."

We climbed out and thanked the friendly Kansas farmer. As he drove off in his battered truck I looked around. Sonuvabitch if weren't back on the very same ramp where he'd picked us up!

Nothing to do but stick out our thumbs again and wait. We finally caught a ride that took us to Wichita. There we decided to take I-35 down to Oklahoma City and then pick up I-40 out of OK City. As time passed we began to notice that there was hardly any traffic. Wichita was a pretty fair-sized city and it was still early in the evening, so this seemed a bit strange. Finally a car stopped and the driver told us to get off the street, as a big tornado was heading our way. Then the guy drove off and left us there. The wind got stronger and then somebody drove by and yelled, "You better get your ass inside! There's a tornado coming!"

We didn't have anywhere to go, so we just sat there. The wind got really fucking strong. Rain was pouring down on us. Finally this stoned dragster freak picked us up, just before the tornado hit. This freak was blasting along at about 100 mph, the wind was going about *200* mph, rain and crap was flying all over the place. I wasn't sure if we were on the highway or were just flying. That car was rocking and rolling! I expected to see Dorothy and Toto fly by at any moment! This nut just kept blasting down the highway until we reached Oklahoma City. Maybe our added weight helped keep the car on the road. We heard on the freak's radio that six people were killed by the tornado back in Wichita.

The kid dropped us off somewhere on I-40 in western Oklahoma. We caught a series of short rides into Texas and finally made it into Albuquerque on Thanksgiving Day, 1973. We headed down to the municipal park, where we hooked up yet again with Lobo, Black Barry, and Cocaine. We all decided to hang out in Albuquerque for a bit and bum up enough for a good Thanksgiving meal. We were all strung out along Central Avenue, panhandling, when some guy gave Black Barry a $20 and told us all go somewhere and get a good Thanksgiving dinner. We all trooped into a nearby restaurant called the Frontier, which I think is still there, and we did exactly that, each of us ordering its Thanksgiving Special.

Even though there were now six of us, we decided to try our luck together, as we were nearing our destination. After a while a hippie in a VW van stopped and picked us all up. Packed into the van with our gear, we all headed down the road, still heading west.

Just after we passed through Grants, New Mexico, the hippie driver stopped to pick up a hippie chick hitching alone on the highway out in the middle of nowhere. The girl turned out to be Kay, who we hadn't seen since we all started out together back in Boston! What the hell? We whooped and hollered and all hugged her and welcomed her back into the tribe. Kay was even happier than us, as she'd been on her own all across the country. She settled in and told us her story.

Her group had soon split up and she and Juan Valez had made it to Pittsburgh, where Juan Valez said he was fed up with hitching. He convinced her that he knew what he was doing, and so they went to the Grayhound bus station in downtown Pittsburgh and tried to sneak onto a bus to Albuquerque. They busted Juan, but Kay managed to disappear among the passengers on the bus, which she rode all the way to Albuquerque. From there she hitched to Grants, where she stayed for a few days with a cousin and recuperated from the road. Then she headed out on the road again.

And then some van full of scruffy street people pulled over for her. She climbed into the van, and discovered that she'd found her tribe once again, about 3,000 miles down the road. Again, what were the odds? It had to be the cosmos looking out for us.

The hippie in the van dropped us all off in Flagstaff, Arizona. We conferred and agreed to split up in order to get rides down to Phoenix, our goal. We'd find each other in the suburb of Tempe, home of Arizona State University, somewhere on Mill

Avenue, the main street. It wasn't that long a street, and we'd have no trouble hooking up. Like Berkeley's Telegraph Avenue, or Cambridge's Harvard Square, it was the place to be if you were in that college town.

Each group took its turn catching rides, with Sally, Maybe, and me going last. I don't know how Lobo and Co. got a ride, but me, Sally, and Maybe got a ride with some *nuts!* Two damn drunken cowboys with their Easy Rider rifle racks in the rear window. They drove their pickup all over the road while the three of us huddled in the back, beer cans flying out the windows.

It's only 120 miles from Flagstaff down to Phoenix, a three-hour drive at most, so by that night all of us were sauntering along together along Mill Avenue. Our little band of gypsies had made it from Boston back to the Desert Southwest and we were ready to party hardy in that warmer clime!

Desert Sojourn

On Mill Avenue that night we ran into STP Family members Governor and Kenny Redport. Kenny's last name wasn't actually "Redport." He went by that name because he favored Red Port wine, a cheap wine favored by winos, and Kenny definitely loved that cheap wine. Governor, though, loved Thunderbird, another cheap wine, and always had one of those suede wineskins filled with Thunderbird slung over his shoulder. We had become pretty good friends the previous summer in Earth Peoples Park back in Vermont. Kenny was a huge Dylan fan and was always asking me to play this or that Dylan song.

Kenny and Governor were up from Tucson to sneak into a Grateful Dead concert in Phoenix. We all decided to head to the Dead concert together. The previous summer a large group of STPers were at the big Watkins Glen concert in New York where the Dead acknowledged the STP family from the stage, so we thought there was a good chance we could all get in free.

Somehow we convinced the general concert security to let us backstage and we met the head of the Dead's security. He passed a message to Jerry Garcia that the STP family was in attendance and asked about us getting in free. Well, I don't know what happened since Watkins Glen, but the word came back that NO ONE from the STP family was to be allowed into the concert. So much for the free Grateful Dead concert.

But, while we were banned from the Dead concert, we wanted to party together, which was the big goal of every day on the street, so we got some liquor. Then we had to decide on a place to party hardy.

There was an entire community of street people in Tempe at that time. The dry Salt River bed was the border between Phoenix and Tempe and they were strung out all along the bank of the Salt River bed in tents and bush hovels at a small municipal park on the Phoenix side. It was like an old hobo jungle from the Great Depression. We could have found a place to party there, but we wanted a more comfortable location.

I was born and raised in Phoenix, so I had family there. My younger brother Dennis and my older brother Bruce were sharing an apartment in Phoenix on the edge of the Papago Park desert. They were at a sleazy complex we called the "Erotica Motel," although that wasn't its actual name. We called it that because it was cheap and guests used it for a few hours of a mid-day rendezvous with hookups. It was on the eastern edge of Phoenix at the corner 52nd Street and Van Buren and was managed by two longhaired potheads who looked the other way at the various shenanigans at the Erotica.

These guys were total stoners. My younger brother Pat was a sophomore at East High at this time and, although he had long hair and all, he wasn't as fully into the life that we were, or even as the stoners were. One time they invited him to sit with them in their office and smoke some ganja weed which, they told him, was laced with opium. It was the first time he smoked opium and Pat said the opium totally befuddled him. He was like one of those Chinese opium addicts that you see in old movies lying zonked out in an opium den. There was a Circle K convenience store across the street from the motel and, after smoking up, he went over there to buy a Big Gulp. He said he stood staring at the dispenser for what seemed to be an eternity. He just stood there, staring at the nozzles in a semi-coma. Finally the clerk yelled for him to either buy something or get out of the store.

He ambled out of the store, but then couldn't figure out how to get across the street. There was too much traffic. He figured he'd wait until the traffic lessened, but it never seemed to lessen, so he just stood there at the side of the road, in his opium coma, for another eternity.

Anyway, since the Erotica Motel wasn't that far from Mill Avenue, I suggested we pay my brothers a visit. Dennis was excited and enthralled by the road rabble that suddenly appeared at his door and took over his home, but Brother Bruce was not. By that time we were all liquored up and were pretty raucous. Governor, who was black, took exception to the large Confederate battle flag Bruce had hanging on his living room wall. "What the fuck is that racist flag doing hanging on your wall?" he demanded. "I'm going to tear that fucker down."

"The hell you are," Bruce said, standing in his way to protect his rebel flag. "This is my place and that's my flag, and you're not going to touch it!" Our family had a Southern heritage. Mom was born and raised in Chattanooga, Tennessee, as was Bruce. We had family back there, and Bruce had just come back to Phoenix from spending time with the Southern branch of the family. One of our cousins had given Bruce the rebel flag as a parting gift, and he was determined to protect the family heirloom. "You touch this flag and I'll punch you in the face!" He clenched his fists and glowered at Governor. The two were just getting ready to go at each other over the rebel flag when events in the bathroom interrupted them.

Lobo and Cocaine, both drunk as lords, had squirreled up in the bathroom and were fucking loudly. Lobo had hoisted Cocaine up on the bathroom sink and was fucking her standing up. Her weight, however, broke the sink out of the wall, and water began spraying all over the room. But, Lobo and Cocaine just kept fucking on the floor, water spewing all over them.

That stopped Bruce and Governor's incipient civil war over the Confederate battle flag and focused all of our drunken attention. "That's it!" Bruce yelled, waving his arms. "Everybody out! I want everybody out of my house, right now! Get the hell out!"

Lobo and Cocaine finished fucking in the flooding bathroom and we all slowly shuffled out, with Bruce yelling hysterically and jumping around to herd us out. "Don't you ever bring these people back here," Bruce growled at me as we left.

"OK, I fucking won't," I replied. "Sorry, Bro. We were just trying to have some fun."

"Have your fun someplace else. But don't come back here again."

So, we all headed back to Mill Avenue. We wandered around Tempe for the next few days, hanging out with various lowlifes we encountered along the avenue. A guy named Chino and his girlfriend, Motor Mouth, began running with us for a while. They were always fighting in public, and Motor Mouth would start crying and yelling, "Chino,

Chino, Chino!" They split up, and Motor Mouth began hanging with our road rabble. And so passed the first days of December.

Eventually, we all began to tire of Tempe. One night we all got drunk and Sally and I got into an argument about something. I threw my mule skinner knife at her and it stuck in the wall about three inches above her head. She was afraid I was gonna kill her, so she and Kay and Cocaine decided to head up to Taos and hook up with some people they knew there in a commune. Black Barry, Lobo, and I, along with Maybe and Motor Mouth, decided to drift on down to Tucson and spend some time with the STP Family down there. So, the trio of girls left for Taos, and the rest of us headed for Tucson.

The house where Governor and Kenny Redport were staying was owned by a woman named Patty and was crammed full of street riff-raff. Many of them, like Asshole Dave, Kenny Redport's traveling partner, we already knew. It was a good place to hang, with a party every night, so we hung out in Tucson for quite a while.

We started doing all the things you did with STPers: Raising hell, tearing Tucson apart, getting kicked out, coming back, getting drunk, passing out, getting pissed on, waking up, stinking, shaking with the DTs. All we did was panhandle and drink gallons of wine and drop acid. We were constantly freaked out, totally incoherent. We were getting to be the real dregs of society. There's a saying, "If you can remember the Sixties (or, in our case, the early Seventies), you weren't really there." That's true for a lot of us. I later met some of the people I knew on the road, and God alone knows how many brain cells they lost. Their minds were totally burned out from drugs and booze. Suprisingly, though, some of them became succesful and productive members of society.

Because we had a well-deserved reputation for being drugged up all the time, nice clean-cut college kids sometimes sought us out as their drug connections. One time, when Lobo and I were hanging out in Albuquerque's Yale Park, two college kids hit us up for some acid. I pulled out a small plastic pill box and showed the contents to them. "This will definitely send you on a trip," I said.

"How much for all of them?" one asked.

"$20."

The two conferred, and each coughed up $10 and I gave them the pills.

The next night they came back with some of their buddies. "Wow! That was some good stuff you sold us," one of my previous customers said. "We were wondering if you had any more for my friends, here."

"Well," I said, "not at this very moment, but if you'll hang on a bit, I know where to get some."

"OK, we'll wait."

So Lobo and I sauntered down to the local convenience store and bought another bottle of saccahrine pills for my good customers.

One night when we were in Albuquerque, a really ugly girl named Onica, along with Lobo and me, got some acid. We all went to Onica's house and dropped it. Her acid trip turned Onica on and she wanted to fuck Lobo. He didn't want to have anything to do with her, so he said he to go get some booze, and left.

I was zonked out on a couch on Onica's front porch. Onica shook me awake and asked if I wanted to fuck. Her looks turned me off just as much as they had Lobo, so I told her that sounded good, but I was hungry as hell, and wondered if she had some food first. She didn't, but said she'd get some. She left to buy some burritos at a store across the street. While she was gone, I took off to find Lobo.

I found Lobo at the park where we all hung out and told him I was pissed that he left me there alone with Onica. He just laughed.

"Yeah, well you can laugh now, motherfucker, but I told Onica that you told me you really liked her, and you wanted her to meet you tomorrow here in the park. I'll be the one laughing when she shows up and starts pawing all over you!"

Then, up came Onica with the burritos. "Still hungry?" she asked. And it was indeed my turn to laugh.

One day Kenny was hanging out in Tucson's central park with us, where we spent most of the time we were down there. Like all of us, Kenny was panhandling in order to scrape together enough for some wine. Sometimes, though, he bought a sandwich instead, since even a wino can't live entirely on wine. Sometimes he even had enough to buy an extra sandwich, which he'd leave in the fridge back at the communal house so he'd have something to eat when he came home. However, even though he put his name on his sandwich, sometimes he'd come home to find it gone, or half of it gone. He demanded to know who the hell was eating his sandwich but, of course, no one ever 'fessed up.

So, one day Kenny decided to wreak his revenge. He took a nice juicy turd of his shit and spread it thickly over two slices of brown bread like it was peanut butter. Then he wrapped it tightly and neatly in Saran Wrap and put his name on it. Then he placed it on the top shelf of the fridge and went out for the day to panhandle. When he came home that night, he found his sandwich in the fridge unwrapped, with a big bite taken out of it. Kenny had gotten his revenge. He cackled like hell when he told us that story. Kenny later put a shotgun in his mouth up in San Francisco and blew the top of his head off.

By then Lobo and Black Barry and I had been in Tucson for about two or three weeks, and we were drinking wine all the time, all day and all night. We were constantly drunk and we were beginning to wake up every morning with the shakes. We decided to get the hell out of there before we became complete alcoholics. We caught rides back up to Phoenix, with an intention of going on to Berkeley. I thought Abbe, a girl I'd met at Earth People's Park in Vermont and liked a lot, might be at the Earth People's House in Berkeley.

So, the three of us took off and were walking down Telegraph Avenue in Berkeley within two days. It was December of '73, and the Avenue was really dead, so we headed for the Earth People's house, but Abbe wasn't there. In fact, hardly anyone was there, and those who were didn't welcome us. They considered us to be members of the STP Family, which they considered to be too rowdy, and so they invited us to leave. Even so, they let us spend Christmas with them. We managed to cop some acid, which we instantly dropped, so we had a colorful Christmas Day. They let us eat the remains of their Christmas dinner. Very generous of them.

The next day, since Berkeley was so dead, we said, "Fuck it" and headed back to Phoenix, which we reached in only a day and a half. Black Barry ran into a girl, Anita, that he'd been spending time with previously, so we crashed at her place in Tempe. She had a little kid, and Black Barry and Anita began to get really tight.

We spent the days cruising Mill Avenue, and a young girl began hanging with us, or at least Lobo. One night the cops stopped Lobo and the girl as they were sauntering down the Avenue. They said the girl was a runaway and the girl's father was going to press statutory rape charges against Lobo, because the girl was only 16. Of course, this was just bullshit from the cops. Nothing would have come of it anyway, because Lobo was only 17 himself. None of us were legally adults, because none of us were over 18. And all of us were runaways, from somewhere.

One day we ran into a girl I used to go to East High with, and she invited us to a party at a place called "Brothers' Lake." It wasn't actually a lake, just a spot of desert oasis on the far side of the Phoenix Zoo, which was itself located in or on the edge of Papago Park. We never turned down an invitation to party, so we headed on over.

When we arrived, there were already about 30 people there and, for a while, we had a good time. Then, about an hour or so after we arrived, a bunch of cowboys showed up and began causing trouble. By then we were all as drunk as skunks, and we heard people buzzing excitedly that there was going to be a fight. Black Barry and I followed the crowd to see the fight, and we found Lobo and some cowboy mixing it up in the middle of a ring of shouting and laughing people. Lobo was kicking the cowboy's ass, so some of the cowboys jumped in to pile up on Lobo.

Naturally, Black Barry and I jumped in, and then some more cowboys jumped us. Things turned into a general melee, with flailing fists and grappling bodies. Before I knew it, I was on the ground and a cowboy was kicking me in the side with his pointy-toed boot. Black Barry came to my rescue with a limb he'd ripped off a tree. He swung it around like a berserker, and the cowboys who were pummeling me took off.

Then Lobo came out of the dark with blood gushing down his face. Black Barry dropped the tree limb and pulled out the hatchet he always carried at his waist, and I remembered that I had my mule skinner knife in a sheath on my belt. I pulled it out and the three of us began shouting insults at the cowboys. Because we were waving our weapons at them, they wouldn't come near us, but they began stoning us from a distance. There were too many of them for us to charge them, so we decided to retreat. The cowboys were like a pack of dogs trailing after us and harassing us. As soon as we turned our backs on them, they'd come running up, and we'd have to whirl and face them and threaten them with our weapons until they backed off.

We crossed the highway from Papago Park into the parking lot of an amusement park called Legend City. We approached some people parked in the lot and told them a gang of cowboys had jumped us. We asked if they could give us a ride to a hospital emergency room, as it seemed Lobo's nose was broken. They drove us all to the county hospital, where a doctor fixed Lobo's nose while we waited for him. Lobo returned in good spirits and told us the doctor shoved two Q-Tips dipped in cocaine up his nose, and then set his nose and put a splint on it. That was Lobo's story, anyway.

A few days after that we ran into one of the kids we'd met at the party in the park and we asked him who the hell those cowboys were who'd jumped us. He said they were just a bunch of assholes that partied at Brothers' Lake all the time. We decided to go back that night and ambush them. We got a shotgun and our plan was to hold them all up and kick the shit out of them one by one. We returned to Brothers' Lake with the shotgun every Friday and Saturday night for two weeks, but the cowboys never showed. Perhaps the word got out that we were waiting for them, and they didn't want to argue with a shotgun.

By then we were all staying at Anita's house in Tempe and going every night to a Mill Avenue bar named Perry's. Sally and Kay returned from Taos, without Cocaine, who decided to stay behind. That was the last time we ever saw Cocaine, but I heard later that she got off the streets and became a respectable middle-class matron.

It's too bad Kay didn't stay behind, as she was always getting us into trouble. One night, for instance, all of us except for Kay and her cousin Billy (remember, Kay was originally from Tempe) were drinking in some dark bushes behind a house with a big picture window. Suddenly Kay and cousin Billy came running up to us out of breath. It seems Kay had been standing at the picture window staring at the guy inside who was watching TV. He looked up and saw Kay staring at him and Kay, for some unknown reason, took offense, yelled at him, and smashed the window with her fist.

Soon after that an army of cops surrounded us, with lights flashing and guns drawn. They lined us up and took our pictures. They thought Sally and Lobo were the ones who broke the guy's picture window, but the homeowner couldn't identify them as the ones. They had to let us go, but after that the Tempe cops had us marked, and they began to constantly hassle us. There was one cop who walked a beat on Mill Avenue, and he told us he didn't want to see us on his side of the street, ever.

Meanwhile, Lobo had hooked up with a girl named Stella that he liked a lot. She was a mountain lady, and Lobo had always talked a lot about leaving the city and losing himself up in the mountains. He came from Colorado and loved the Rockies. They began talking about going back to the land, and the idea began to seem increasingly appealing to all of us.

One night Lobo, Black Barry, and I went into a bar on the avenue to drink and shoot pool. Two Tempe cops came into the bar and busted all three of us for wearing knives in a bar, which they said was illegal. They hauled us off to the Tempe jail and we appeared in court before a judge the next day. At that time Lobo was going under the name of "Cole Younger," and the judge asked him if he was related to the infamous outlaw of yore. Lobo said he wasn't sure.

As I said, Phoenix was my hometown, so my mother came to the court that day to plead on our behalf. We were released into her custody after promising to find jobs so that we could either pay the fine for carrying knives in the bar, or get the hell out of town.

Well, it wasn't the first time we'd been ordered to get out of town. It wasn't even the first time we'd been ordered to get out of my hometown. It happened a lot. The previous year, for instance, we'd been paraded out of Cloudcroft, New Mexico. We had over-stayed our welcome at the house of these two dudes who wanted to fuck Willa and Kay-Kay, the girls we were with. The girls weren't willing, so the dudes called the cops to have us evicted.

The cops came, made us gather up our shit, and then paraded us down the road to downtown Cloudcroft. They marched us in front of their cruiser as they rolled along behind us at about three mph, lights flashing. Cloudcroft was a dinky little town and there wasn't much to it, or much to see, so people lined up on both sides of the street to see the cops parading the road rabble out of town. The girls who were with us began flashing their boobs and other parts of their bodies, shocking the old ladies who were gawking at us. I looked back expecting the high school marching band to join us, perhaps some baton twirlers, and maybe some Shriner clown cars.

After we paraded about a mile out of town the cops stopped following us and said on their loudspeaker, "If you know what's good for you, you won't come back to Cloudcroft." I had the urge to moon the cops, but I knew which end of the stick I was on, and that would have only led to jail, so I didn't drop my pants.

There was a game these towns played with us. Many times the cops in these small towns would bust us for some trumped up charge, such as vagrancy, loitering, or breathing, and keep us in jail for a few days. Then some legal official would visit us. He'd tell us that we could plead no contest to a reduced charge, and get time served and immediately released, on the condition that we leave town and never come back.

Or we could stay in jail a few months awaiting a trial, because we had no bail money. Then, at trial, we'd undoubtedly be found guilty of vagrancy, loitering, or breathing, and perhaps sentenced to even more time in jail.

Well, we weren't idiots, so we took the deal and left town. But, by then it was getting to be hard to remember all the small towns across the country from which we were banned. It seemed there were fewer and fewer places left in America where we could just live and be ourselves.

Back to the Land

After being ordered out of Tempe, we decided to take off for Taos, even though Sally said the Taos cops had given her and Cocaine a lot of shit while they were there. Cocaine had been kicked out of a bar up there for being loud and rowdy. She didn't take kindly to that, so she went back with a meat cleaver and chased the asshole she said had harassed her all around the bar with the cleaver. Of course, the cops were called, and they busted both Cocaine and Sally. While they were in the Taos jail, one of the cops felt up Sally's tits. Sally complained to the county prosecutor, and he gave the cops at the jailhouse a lot of shit. This did not endear Sally and Cocaine to the Taos cops.

Despite this, we all decided to return to Taos, as we'd become fed up with Tempe. We all caught a ride up to Flagstaff, and were dropped off in that mountain town at night. It was February of '74 and it was snowing and it was cold as hell, so we all decided to go into a restaurant called Little America and get some coffee and warm up. We settled into a booth and, while waiting for the waitress to come by, I read the story of Little America on the back of the menu. According to that story, a long time ago a sheepherder was caught out in the wilderness by a blizzard and wished he had a warm place to go where he could get a cup of coffee. So, he founded Little America as a friendly and warm place for cold travelers on cold nights.

Well, that story was a load of bullshit. We waited for about an hour for the waitress to come by our booth. When she finally did come by, she turned out to be a real bitch. We got our coffee, but then she wouldn't come by to give us our free refills. We decided sit there in that restaurant until we got our free refills. The hours went by, and finally the waitress came over and said we had to leave.

"We're not leaving until we get our free refills of coffee," I told her.

"I'm not serving you any more coffee. You have to leave."

"No, we're going to sit here until you give us our coffee."

"Then I'm calling the cops."

"You do that."

So the Flagstaff cops came and told us we all had to clear out of warm and friendly Little America, and, in fact, get the hell out of Flagstaff.

We grumbled about that, but we gathered our stuff and left Little America. "Thanks for nothing," I yelled at the waitress as the cops escorted us out into the dark night.

But, we were lucky out on the road, and by morning we were all in Albuquerque, then up to Santa Fe, then on to Taos. There we ran into some of Sally's old friends and they said we could stay with them for a while. They lived in a small house about a block from the town's center plaza. After that we moved around from house to house. Sally had worked for a silversmith named Frank for a while, and we ran into him and spent a night at his house up in Questa. Most of the time, as always on the road, we just hung out and partied.

Lobo came originally from Denver, and we were near the Colorado border, so Lobo decided to drop by his old homestead for a visit. He called his sister, who sent him bus money, and he left for home.

After he left we ran into old friends Beverly and Jim, who were now living in Arroyo Hondo, so we visited them. They were an odd pair. Jim was a big and tall Indian and lived like an old mountain man. Bev, on the other hand, was very small, it seemed she was like four-feet tall. They lived in a cave everyone called "Preacher's Cave" in the side of a small cliff, about two miles from the highway and up a little stream. You had to walk all the way to their place over rough ground, because there was no road. The steep path was about two-feet wide and was about 30-feet above a small stream called the Rio Hondo. It was a nice and peaceful place, and so we stayed in Preacher's Cave with them for about a week. We were completely away from civilization, as if we'd stepped back in time.

One night we were sitting around the fire just outside the cave, surrounded by the black night, with a billion stars in the dark sky above us. We could see nothing beyond the firelight, but Jim could. Suddenly he grabbed up the rifle by his side and fired off into the night. A deer that had come down to the stream to drink tumbled down into the stream. Jim picked up his big Bowie knife and went out to get the deer. He dragged it back to the fire, butchered it, and we all had deer meat to eat that night. We ate the heart first to honor the kill.

By this time we were all pretty fed up with living on the street, being constantly hassled by the cops and all the good citizens, and being run out of town after town. We began to long for an isolated place in the mountains, like Arroyo Hondo, where we could just live in peace. Earth People's Park in Vermont had been like that for a while, but Lobo and I loved the Rocky Mountains, and that's where we wanted to be.

Lobo returned from Denver after about two weeks and said he couldn't relate to any of the people he used to know there in his previous life. Their entire lives were now alien to him. I'd already experienced that with my own family and former friends, so I knew exactly what he meant. It was like the lives of our families and old friends were all pre-programed and they were just plodding along, mindlessly living the program.

Meanwhile, all of us out on the road were living outside of normal society, outside of our times. We agreed that all of us should have been born in the early 1800s, so we could just go off into the Rockies and be Mountain Men. All of us on the streets were like a giant rabble of misplaced people, lost in time, wandering back and forth across America from coast to coast, just trying to survive and live our lives. But, America didn't want us and wouldn't let us be, and we felt helpless to fight back against our ever-increasing enemies.

Then Lobo told me about some land out in the woods that his stepfather owned up in northern Idaho. He suggested that we could head up there and start a rural commune like Earth People's Park. That sounded like a good idea because, by then, we'd come to the conclusion that we had to either get off the road, or die. And we weren't willing to die just yet.

So, we decided to head off into the mountains, and become the Mountain Men we all thought we should be anyway. But, instead of heading straight for Idaho, we decided to return to Earth People's Park in Vermont instead. We wanted to gather the tribe.

But, before we could head out of town we had to have one more party. Saint Paddy's Day was upon us and we heard there was going to be a large party at film star Dennis Hopper's house. He owned the large complex that had once been owned by a rich transplant from New York named Mable Dodge Luhan. She was the one who urged her artistic friends to move from New York to Taos at the turn of the century, and she was thus mainly responsible for turning Taos into an artists' mecca. Her place, which became Dennis Hopper's place, is now a very expensive bed and breakfast.

Anyway, we'd heard about the party at Dennis Hopper's place from a guy we met in the plaza who went by the moniker of Striker. Talking to this guy I found out he was born and raised in Phoenix and, not only that, but he was from my own neighborhood. After further discussion it turned out this guy was an old schoolmate and friend of my brother Bruce, who now lived at the Erotica Motel. I remembered his name as Harry, before he became "Striker."

So, we all trekked over to Dennis Hopper's place, which had been Mabel Dodge Luhan's place. The little walled adobe patio was full of people, and the drugs and liquor were flowing freely. We never did see Hopper, and he may not have even been there.

Around two in the morning, Lobo, Striker and I were standing next to one of the adobe walls pissing on the wall. All of a sudden, Striker bent over and cupped his hands under my stream of warm steaming piss, filled his hands, and started slurping it. Now, we were used to seeing some weird shit, but this was just a little too bizarre for me. We quickly ditched Brother Bruce's old school buddy.

We left the party and, since it was getting toward dawn, went to crash at Frank's shop. Frank was the silversmith Sally worked for sometimes. Early the next morning Frank came in ranting and yelling. "What the fuck did you guys do? This is not cool. You guys got to get the fuck out of my place. The cops are looking all over for you."

Lobo and I looked at each other, going over the events of the night before and not remembering anything spectacular. It turned out, though, that someone had liberated some Native American artifacts from the local museum, and the word was out that we did it.

We'd made friends with probably the only black resident in Taos, a guy named Clinton, who had a large ranch outside Taos. Black Barry had been staying there (we thought he had the hots for Clinton's girlfriend), so we decided that Lobo would lay low at Clinton's ranch, while Sally and I would head down to Santa Fe to figure out our next step.

As soon as we got to Santa Fe we ran into a guy who let us crash at his old adobe not far from the plaza. We hung out for about a week and then figured it was cool enough to head back up to Taos. We stuck out our thumbs and were picked up by three longhaired guys in pickup with a camper on the back. They were headed to up Taos and they seemed to be cool, so we informed them of our situation.

When we got to Taos they drove us over to Clinton's, where we hooked up with Black Barry and Lobo. Our new friends were two brothers named Ruff and Ready, and a guy named Star. They had heard about Earth People's Park and were planning on making a trek out east in a month or so. Heading for the park seemed like something they'd be interested in doing. In the meantime, they were heading to California to meet up with some people, including Star's wife, and invited us to go with them.

Well, a venture to the East was much better when it was warmer, so we decided to go with them before heading east. Black Barry decided to stay there. He was in love with Clinton's wife. We wished him good luck with that, and that was the last time we saw Black Barry.

We all piled into the camper and, in a couple days, we all arrived at this large house in Sylmar, California. In the backyard of this house were several trailers and camper shells up on cement blocks. There we met Bill, who lived in a large trailer in that backyard with his girlfriend, the daughter of the people who owned the property, and who lived in the house in front. It turned out that Bill was a jewelry thief who had cases and cases of hot jewels stashed around his trailer.

After a couple of weeks of living in those trailers, I was becoming a little paranoid. The parents up front didn't like us, and I was worried about cops raiding this place, hunting the jewelry thief, and getting caught up in it. The last thing I wanted was to be in some southern California jail. Lobo and I talked about it, and we agreed that Sally and I would head back East to Earth People's Park, and he would follow with Ruff and Star and Star's wife, Mary, a week later.

Sally and I hitched to Phoenix to say goodbye to my Mom. We ran into Kay there, who was still hanging out on Mill Avenue, and she wanted to come with us, so the three of us hit the road.

We made it up to Flagstaff, where a guy in a VW van picked us up. He had a shaved head, and he didn't take long to volunteer that he was AWOL from the army. Kay nicknamed him Knucklehead, because he didn't seem to know what the hell he was doing. We told him about Earth People's Park, and he decided he wanted to go with us, so we had a ride all the way to our destination.

Earth People's Park was crowded with a lot of old friends. Black TC was there, living with his new old lady, Denise. Beverly and Jim from Arroyo Hondo showed up. Bev was now pregnant and about to give birth. We told everyone about our idea of setting up a western Earth People's Park in the backwoods of Idaho on the land belonging to Lobo's stepdad, and some of them wanted to come with us.

By this time we'd begun acquiring weapons. I obtained an old cap and ball .44 and some blasting caps. TC had a double-barreled 12-gauge shotgun, which he traded to Jim for a nickel-plated .38. TC then traded the .38 for an 8mm Mauser rifle. Then TC wanted my .44, so I traded it to him for his Mauser rifle, which is what I really wanted, anyway. Star, who finally arrived from California with Mary, Lobo, and Ruff, had several rifles, and so he gave Ruff, a 7.7 Jap sniper rifle, and he gave Lobo a 20-gauge shotgun. He kept a 30-40 Krag rifle for himself, so we were all well armed.

We wanted hunting weapons for our projected Idaho retreat. However, we were also getting tired of taking endless shit from the cops, year after year, and we were all near the breaking point. Acquiring the guns just seemed to be a natural evolution. While we were at Earth People's Park, the LAPD massacred the Symbionese Liberation Army back in California. Soon after that, a police chopper went down in Sylmar, where we'd been staying. The SLA claimed to have shot it down in retaliation for the massacre. It seemed like a war was erupting in America, and what happened to the SLA could happen to us. We wanted to be ready for anything.

Then we had to decide who was going to make the trek with us to our new mountain home in the Rockies. Jim and pregnant Bev were building a house near the old A-Frame that I used to live in with Abbe, so they were going to stay at Earth People's Park. Kay was also going to stay there. But TC and Denise wanted to go with Lobo, Sally, and me. Ruff decided to come, along with Star and his wife, Mary, who was also hugely pregnant. All together, there were ten of us, along with two dogs. We crammed into a van, along with all our crap, and headed out.

We decided to go west by way of Canada, since Earth People's Park was right there on the border. We had no trouble crossing the border into Canada and, after spending the night in a Montreal youth hostel, headed west. As we crossed Canada the cops stopped us a few times, but we had no problems. We hid our weapons under a mattress that pregnant Mary laid on and moaned when cops pulled us over.

We reached the province of Alberta soon enough and crossed the border back into the United States at a small place called Sweetgrass, Montana. There we had a small problem. None of us had great I.D., and some of us had none. The Border Patrol told all of us to get out of the van except for pregnant Mary, who was moaning and groaning on her mattress. TC had no I.D. at all, and at first we thought the Border Patrol wasn't going to allow him back into his own country. They asked him all these bullshit questions about American baseball teams, just like they did back in World War II, which none of us could answer. But, they finally let him go, and we all piled into the van and took off.

Our small wandering tribe, comprised of two dogs and ten people, with an eleventh on the way, drove through Glacier National Park and into the Rocky Mountains of northern Idaho. We arrived on the summer solstice, 1974, which seemed to us to be a propitious day. We were eager to escape civilization, disappear into the mountains, and return to the land.

We discovered, however, that escaping civilization and returning to the land wasn't as easily accomplished as we'd hoped. Civilization soon followed us up into the mountains.

But, that's another story, for another day.

If you enjoyed this story, and want to learn more
about what brought the road rabble to this point, you
can find that story in:

Orphans of the Storm:
A Shared Memoir of the Radical Seventies
By
Morgan M. Morgan, et al.